T0195006

ONLY
God

GAIL GOODWIN

WESTBOW
PRESS®
A DIVISION OF THOMAS NELSON
& ZONDERVAN

WestBow Press books may be ordered through booksellers or by contacting:

WestBow Press
A Division of Thomas Nelson & Zondervan
1663 Liberty Drive
Bloomington, IN 47403
www.westbowpress.com
844-714-3454

All Scripture quotations are taken from the King James Version.

ISBN: 978-1-6642-8773-0 (sc)
ISBN: 978-1-6642-8774-7 (hc)
ISBN: 978-1-6642-8772-3 (e)

Library of Congress Control Number: 2022923698

Print information available on the last page.

WestBow Press rev. date: 02/17/2023

This book is dedicated
to the work of
Our Lord and Savior.
May it be used by Him to
help us find Him
as the Lord of our lives
on our journey homeward.

CONTENTS

ACKNOWLEDGEMENT

Words cannot express my gratitude to my sister, Brenda Clark, who has always been my greatest encourager to keep me moving forward. My lifelong friend Betty Winters, her help has been invaluable. The hours she spent proofreading. She is my prayer partner.

I also wish to show my appreciation to my Pastor, Bro. David Johnson for his time on the book and his prayers and support. Bro. Aaron Middleton's work toward marketing, advice, and support has been vital to publishing this book.

INTRODUCTION

We are searching for answers. Answers to questions that seemed to have none. But there is an answer. It is all in one book. It is called the Bible. When our lives seem out of control, there is always hope. A hope that only God could enforce.

In <u>Only God,</u> we see how to have a personal relationship with God, and as the world steps further and further away from God, we will see how to have peace that only God can give. There is no problem too big for God.

<u>Only God</u> helps us recognize when our greatest enemy, Satan, is trying to lead us away from God.

CHAPTER

The Creator

"In the beginning, God created the heaven and the earth." (King James Version Genesis 1:1). Have you ever looked at a rose? With so many petals, the design has been copied many times, especially in cake decorations making rosettes. It takes layers of petals to make a rose. Some roses have long stems, but all have thorns, just like our lives. Sometimes beautiful, then the thorns show up. The rose has also been used in medicinal cooking and decoration. It is the oldest species of plant to be grown as decoration.

Only after we have cut down a tree can we see how old it is. The rings within the tree tell its history. It also speaks of the climate in which it grew. (The storms of life it survived).

The sunflower faces the sun in the morning. As the sun rises in the east, the flower will stand tall, and as the day progresses, it follows the sun until the evening. It then faces the west, following the sun all day and night. Through the night, it will turn eastward, ready for the new day. Watch in the morning and remember to look again that night the next time the sunflowers bloom. This is a beautiful example of how we should follow the Son. (Jesus)

One of the most beautiful and calm places is sitting on the water's edge. So many things are happening; the ducks are swimming, birds are flying overhead, the fish are sometimes jumping, the winds are blowing the water, or the water becomes a mirror perfectly still. The sounds the water can make!

I was at the lake early one morning in the middle of winter. The temperatures were just below freezing, but the sunrise was beautiful. The colors would take your breath, as would that wind blowing across those icy waters. There was no soul around, but as I stood there looking at the sky, I kept hearing something. It sounded like tiny bells.

The wind blew so hard that the water was almost white, but I could hear the tiniest bells again as the wind died. I walked closer to the water's edge and looked over, and there was my sound. A large patch of sage grass had grown at the bank, now all brown and bending low into the water. Each stalk was covered in ice balls, and as the waves broke on the bank, each crystal of ice would bump against the other ones creating that tiny bell sound. Had there been any noise other than the wind, I would have never heard them.

As we age, we are like the brown sage grass in our last life stage. We may bend low, but we can still create beautiful sounds like those ice crystal bells. We can still be vital witnesses for God. He has a purpose for each of us, no matter our age.

I also love how the wind sounds in the trees. Sometimes it can be a rustling sound as the leaves are moved one against the other. However, the wind can become extraordinarily strong and can warn that storms are close by and to take cover. There was once an old song that asked the question, "Where goes the wind?"

One of my favorite times on the lake is in the evening when the wind is blowing ever so gently across the water, and the sun is setting. It appears as if sparkling diamonds are floating on the water. If we take the time to look, life is all around us. We know this is God's work; He is here every day when the sun rises and sets. Only God could create such beauty.

People have traveled and seen beautiful sights on this earth, such as the northern lights, the Grand Canyon, and the wild mustangs still running free. But we do not have to travel far to see God's creation. Just look in the mirror. Look out the window at a tree. No one can make a tree.

God created all this beauty, and on the sixth day of creation, mankind was made, "So God created man in his own image, in the image of God created he him; male and female created he them." (Genesis 1:27).

Man is the caretaker of this earth. Everything God has created has a purpose: the trees, the flowers, the birds, the animals, the oceans, the rivers, the grass, the mountains, the flat lands, everything. Each creation works together with the next; no oceans exist without rivers, lakes, and streams. Without fruit trees, there would be no fruit, no seeds with which to regrow. Without the sun and rain, nothing would grow. Man, animals, trees, flowers, and every living thing would die. But all things were created to replenish this earth to sustain life for millions of years. Only God could create something this magnificent.

We, too, have a purpose. We were not created for our pleasure but to love and serve God. In (Genesis 1:28), we read that He blessed them as soon as He made man and woman. God has a plan for each one of us. He is waiting to pour His blessings on us more than we can imagine.

Of all His creations, man is the only one to have a soul. Man is the only one that will live eternally. God loves man so much that His son died on the cross so that we could have a home with Him throughout all eternity.

God is to have first place in our lives. Without Him, we would not even be here. We were created in the very image of God. He must have first place in our life, and His word says that everything else will be added unto us (Matthew 6:33).

Our creator loves us very much and wants the absolute best for us.

This book may help someone see the beauty in this life and realize that no matter what we face, we are never alone! Jesus is as close as the whisper of His name.

CHAPTER

Getting to Know Him

*I*t is the simplest thing in the world. We either believe the Bible is true or that it is not. However, when you have read that book, you know it is true.

I spoke with many people that believed in the Bible but only up to a point. They said, "It is because a man had written it." I told them God told the man what to write. As we read in 2 Timothy 3:16, "All scripture is given by inspiration of God, and is profitable for doctrine, for reproof, for correction, for instruction in righteousness:" "Oh yes, He did, but man, being man, added his own words too," they said.

I thought about what they said and wondered if they were right; how would a person know which part of the Bible is genuine? Who would decide what is true and what is not?

I thought maybe they did not believe in God. But the next thing they said was that they knew there was a God, but only part of the Bible was genuine. The Bible is the only book that has stood the test of time. We have thousands of ancient books but none as old as this one. The only book in the world that can prove itself true!

We all would have no hope if the Bible were not wholly accurate, none! But it is all true! It is God's infallible unerring word (Acts 1:3). He is the absolute truth!

The Bible says there is a heaven and a literal hell! Every human being has a soul. When we meet death, that soul will enter heaven or hell. "...to be absent from the body, and to be present with the Lord..." (2 Cor.5:8).

We decide while alive where we will spend eternity, Heaven or Hell. To go to heaven, "Jesus saith unto him, I am the way, the truth and the life no man cometh to the Father but by me." (John 14:6). "For by grace we are saved through faith...." (Eph. 2:8–9) Jesus died on that cross for our sins, "... while we were yet sinners, Christ died for us." (Romans 5:8)

Salvation is not complicated. His word says that we are on our way to hell. "For all have sinned and come short of the glory of God;" (Romans 3:23). So, we ask God to forgive us of our sins and give us a home in heaven when we die. "That if thou shalt confess with thy mouth the Lord Jesus, and shalt believe in thine heart that God has raised him from the dead, thou shalt be saved." (Romans 10:9). Immediately, we become a child of His. He saves our soul, and that's what will live eternally, our soul.

To secure our place in hell.
Do Nothing!

Satan was the most beautiful angel that God had created. But Satan wanted it all. He wanted to be Christ. He wanted to be the Supreme being. That's when there was war in heaven, and Satan was cast out and thrown to this earth (Revelation 12:9).

As recorded in Ephesians 2:2, he is called the prince of the power of the air Hell will be his final home; the Bible also says that one-third of the angels followed him. Satan is always looking for new souls to populate his home with.

Hell is where the worm does not die, a place of eternal torture with flames of fire. Mark 9:44, 46, and 48 says, "Where their worm dieth not, and the fire is not quenched." I have read and quoted this verse before. But today is the first time I see that each person in hell has their own set of worms for all eternity! I knew the fire never stops burning you. But the worms! What a horrible place!

God created hell for the devil, his angels, and anyone Satan can convince to deny God. Those who reject God will live with him in hell for all eternity. This a choice we all make. No one is doomed to hell except the one who denies there is a God. Saying all this is not true will not make it any less true. I have been told you believe what you want, and I will believe what I want. We all have that right. These are not my words but God's, and He said there is only one way to Heaven. "Jesus saith unto him, I am the way, the truth, and the life: no man cometh unto the Father, but by me." (John 14:6)

We are told in Luke 16:22–31 that a rich man was clothed in purple and fine linen. There was also a beggar named Lazarus who lay at his gate and was full of sores. Lazarus only wanted to be fed from the crumbs of the rich man's table. One day the beggar died and was carried away to heaven. The rich man also died, and when he opened his eyes, he knew he was in hell. He saw Abraham and Lazarus afar off, and then he knew what he had heard about heaven and hell was true. Sadly, it was too late for him. The rich man begged Abraham to have mercy on him and send Lazarus to dip his finger in water to cool his tongue. The rich man said, "I am tormented in this flame." (Luke 16:24). Abraham reminded him of how he lived on the earth. He had not accepted Jesus as his Savior. Also, Abraham told him there was a great gulf between them, and no one could pass through.

The rich man told Abraham about his five brothers that still lived on the earth and asked him to send someone to warn his brothers about this awful place. Abraham explained to him that they have Moses and the prophets; let them hear them. The rich man replied, "…if one went unto them from the dead, they would repent." Abraham told him that if they did not hear Moses and the prophets, they would not hear one from the dead. (Luke 16:30–31)

Like today, we have people presenting the gospel to us, but sadly, we do not listen. Our decision about salvation is made while we are alive on this earth. After we die, it is too late to decide where we will spend our eternity.

But because of what Jesus did at Calvary, we do not have to go to hell. It is our choice alone to make. As we read in John 14:2, Jesus said, "In my Father's house are many mansions: if it were not so, I would have told you. I go to prepare a place for you." He has room for all of us. In Revelations 4, John tells us of God's throne, and there is a rainbow around it. The new heaven is described in (Revelation 21:9–27). It has gates of pearl and a street of gold; the walls of the building are made of pure jasper. There is no need for the sun, for God is the light.

If we accept Him as our Savior, this will be our eternal home!

"We walk by faith, not by sight." (II Cor. 5:7). "And He said to the woman, thy faith hath saved thee, go in peace." (Luke 7:50). People have no faith in God even though the Bible is true. "But without faith, it is impossible to please Him...." (Hebrews 11:6).

Death will come to all. We must decide whether it is heaven or hell. The choice is ours. Millions have chosen God as their Savior, but millions have done nothing and refused to believe in Jesus. The sin we must ask God to forgive us for is unbelief in His only Son. Even after He has died on the cross for our sins, people will still reject Him as their Savior. So, please don't wait too long to decide. "And as it is appointed unto men once to die but after this the judgment:" (Hebrews 9:27).

Once we have accepted Christ as our Savior, we begin to understand all His promises. It is a joy knowing that we are never alone, even at two am. God is there because we are now His child. Now God is responsible to us never to break even one promise. Have you ever read those promises? I once read that there are 32,000 promises in the Bible. No matter what we may be going through, there is an answer.

God has a plan for each one of us. "…I am come that they might have life, and that they might have it more abundantly." (John 10:10). To know what He has for us, we must study His Word.

Gail Goodwin

Sometimes He can lead us a certain way, but we don't hear him because we want our way. This is when we step out of the will of God. That is a dangerous place to be. Just because we are His child doesn't mean we are perfect. He saved our souls, not our bodies. One day we will have a new body. We were all born in sin, so we will continue to sin if we are in this body. But not the soul, it will sin no more because His blood covers it, and it belongs to Him. "Ye are bought with a price...." (I Cor. 7:23). That price is that He gave His life for us on the cross. What an awful way to die nailed to a cross! "For God so loved the world, that He gave His only begotten Son, that whosoever believeth in him should not perish, but have everlasting life." (John 3:16)

The moment we ask Jesus to save us, the Holy Spirit abides in our hearts. But we do not automatically know all about Jesus. To know Him and His will for our lives, we read His word, attend His services and learn more about Him. Then as we grow closer, we understand how great a love He has for us. All the promises now belong to us, and we know that Jesus can never break a promise.

Life is a journey; we go through trials. But we are not alone. The challenge is to stay close to Him. It can be challenging to do.

In this world where we currently live, so many things can quickly pull us away from God, such as work, home, and the stress of life. But our primary adversary is Satan. He tries to convince us that God is not real and that the Bible is a lie. He is very cunning when he comes at us, for example, turning one against another, a daughter against mother, son against father. Anywhere he can create confusion. When there is fussing and fighting in our life, we know Satan is nearby and doing his job. We are too busy to figure out who is right and wrong. But the next time we find ourselves in a confusing situation, take a step back and remember that God is not the author of confusion, as He said in (1 Cor. 14:33).

Once we are a child of God, Satan cannot get our souls "…and no man is able to pluck them out my Father's hand." (John 10:29)

But he can make our lives miserable if we do not stay close to God. We cannot overcome Satan by ourselves, but with God, we know Satan has no hold on us. "...because greater is He that is in you, than he that is in the world." (I John 4:4)

Satan comes to us in our minds getting us to believe that things are not true. Jesus said, referring to Satan," ...for he is a liar, and the father of it." (John 8:44). We live as we believe. "For as he thinketh in his heart, so is he...." (Proverbs 23:7). One way to know if what we are going through is of God or Satan is if confusion is present. If it is, then it is not coming from God.

Once we know whom we are battling, it is easier to take it to God in prayer and ask Him for the strength we need to overcome Satan again. Then when we step out of God's will and listen more to Satan, God is always there, ready to forgive us if only we ask. Then the peace of God returns. "And the peace of God, which passeth all understanding, shall keep your hearts and minds through Christ Jesus." (Philippians 4:7).

Only God can do this for us.

CHAPTER

3

God is Leading, But I'm Not Listening

*H*ave you ever read the 10 Commandments in Exodus 20? Such as do not lie, steal, take God's name in vain, do not commit adultery, and honor your father and mother.

Those were the guidelines to live by in the Old Testament days. We know that man could not keep them, so God made us a way to come to Him for our salvation. He gave His only Son to die on the cross for our sins and fulfilled the law of Moses. However, those guidelines are still words to live by. These are the ways God expects us to live. From an early age, we start learning right from wrong. Children would say, "The devil made me do it when caught doing something wrong." But the truth is that the devil cannot make us do anything we do not want to do. We all were born in sin and have a sinful nature within us. Salvation does not make us perfect; it secures our home in heaven when we die. Our soul sins no more, but we are still in this sinful body and will continue to sin as long as we are in the body. We still have that rebellious nature that causes us to sin, and sin puts distance between God and us.

Truthfully sometimes it's easier to stay in sin than to confess and ask for forgiveness, which is exactly where Satan wants us to be, in the dark. To ask for forgiveness, we must admit where we messed up and face the truth about ourselves. This is not always an easy thing to do. Satan knows our weaknesses and uses every chance to deceive us into thinking we are justified in our actions even though we know we are wrong. "Therefore to him that knoweth to do good, and doeth it not, to him it is sin." (James 4:17)

One thing is for sure. Sin puts distance between God and us. Because when we allow sin to stay in our lives, we block the blessings God has meant for us to have. God will not shower us with His blessings if we have unconfessed sin. But His forgiveness restores our fellowship with Him. How sad it will be if, when I get to heaven, God says, "Gail, this was your life, and this was the life I had intended for you."

One way Satan works is by using our circumstances to influence our decisions. He certainly comes at us through our minds. When we see a loved one headed in the wrong direction, we do everything we can to help them turn their life around. But it is their choice.

We even go so far as not to admit aloud that anything is wrong. Whether our loved ones or we have a problem with drugs, alcohol, gambling, or whatever it might be, it seems as if when we say it aloud, it becomes a reality and one we must face.

By not admitting the truth to ourselves, we find it easier every day to go on as if nothing is wrong until the next time it happens. Then it reminds us of what we do not want to face. When we know something is wrong, it doesn't go away and get better without confronting it. Because it is a sin, and sin must always be dealt with.

A child of God can never be comfortable allowing sin to stay in our life. The only way to get rid of our sins is to confess to God and ask for His forgiveness. Our Father is always ready to forgive us and restore our relationship with Him when we do that. We serve an awesome God.

Our Father has a plan for each of our lives. He has thousands of blessings He wants to bestow upon us. But God will not give us those blessings if we are unwilling to listen to Him and follow His path. Like when our children do wrong, we do not reward them for wrongdoing. But when they bring home an exceptional report card or do something great, we usually reward them with praise or gifts.

CHAPTER

4

My Sin

I married a man who lived a secret life even from me. I knew he drank a little before we were married, but I thought he had stopped. At least that is what he told me. I loved him very much and was so excited about our future.

We had been dating for one year when he surrendered to preach. We dated another year before we were married. We were both raised in Church, and each had been saved. I was so sure he was the one.

I was so happy. I knew we could be an incredible team and work for our Lord. I was raised to believe that marriage was for life. You take the good with the bad, but you must be committed for life, no matter what.

He was working, and I was still in high school. I was so excited about him working every day to make us a living. I would soon finish school, and then we were off to conquer the world for our Lord.

Sadly, only after a week of marriage I discovered he was lying about where he was spending his days and where the money was going. He had quit his job and was hanging out with friends until time for him to be coming home from work. I was devasted! Only God could show me how to forgive him.

My husband convinced me that once I had forgiven him, it was my responsibility as his wife to be his helpmate and stay with him.

As the years passed, I learned why he only stayed on any one job, usually no longer than two years. Why we were always moving to greener pastures, he was secretly drinking! There were times when it was so bad that I would have to leave with the children and start over. Then, after months of working three jobs and when I was back on my feet, he would always talk me into coming back. I know now it was partly for the money.

He would speak of God often and how we should live, convincing me he had indeed stopped drinking this time. He even preached and pastored churches. To my knowledge, he was not drinking when he was pastoring churches. However, God did use this man in His service souls were saved under his preaching. He had the desire to do what God had called him to do. But somehow, somewhere, something happened, and he didn't always stay with it. As close as I thought I was to him. I didn't know his heart. I cannot speak to what he was thinking.

I ignored those gentle nudges from the Holy Spirit saying, "you know following your husband is wrong." I had convinced myself I was doing the right thing by staying with him. I was a suitable helpmate, as the Bible says. Satan uses God's word against us to get us to disobey God. I was sure I could help him turn things around and return to God.

But this is precisely where I was fooling myself. This is an individual decision each one of us decides for ourselves. We can't make someone else be what we want them to be, no matter how much we care. No matter how heartbreaking.

I was trying to show him where he was wrong. I was trying to tell him he needed to stop all this and get his life straightened out. I talked with him for hours on end. I knew after all these years I could surely reach him. I learned how much he needed me to take care of him. When I would have to leave, his drinking was worse than if I were at home.

Did you notice that almost every sentence in the paragraph above begins with the word I? This was my sin. I tried to fix my marriage by myself. I was trying to get him to see. But this wasn't my place. This is what our Holy Spirit does. The Holy Spirit convicts us when we are wrong, he tells us when we are headed in the wrong direction, and he tells us what God has to say about how we live. My job was to continue to pray for him and let God oversee this.

No matter how much I wanted things to be right this time, they weren't. God wanted me out of the picture, to leave, stay gone, and allow God to work instead of me trying to work things out.

Things were always good for a while when I would leave and come back. He had indeed stopped drinking, and I was so thankful. But before long, maybe a year or two, it would start all over. I would think I smelled liquor on his breath, "No, not again!

He just couldn't!" He would run out of money before payday, become angry over nothing; he would be condensing. There were signs I would ignore and not believe it was starting again.

I can look back now and see a pattern. When we are in the middle of things, we can't always know the truth—another highly effective tool of Satan.

Eventually, I lost faith in my husband, whom I loved with all my heart. With trust gone from the marriage, there is nothing left. You are always suspicious of what he is doing and where he has been. I did not want to admit what he was. But before I knew it, my life had gone by with me trying to fix things and not letting God have control. Even though I had unconfessed sin, God still loved me and helped me every day. The same way we do for our children. Nothing our children can do can make us stop loving them.

There was always turmoil and confusion in my home. God was not in this. By not listening to those gentle nudges from the Holy Spirit, I was sinning against God.

Once, things were so bad that he went to rehab, but while he was there, I met the sweetest lady who told me she was a recovering alcoholic. She said she had overcome her problems with only God's help. She was now sober for many years and was helping others get sober.

I confided in her some of the problems we faced. She replied that she looked at her problems as if they were like an open string of pearls, and each pearl stood for a pain in her life. Remember the commercial that said you are in good hands? It would show a picture of two hands cupped side by side. She imagined those hands were like God's, and she had prayed to the Lord about each of her struggles. She placed each pearl (each problem) into those big, solid, capable hands. Just like He tells us to do in (Matthew 11:28), "Come unto me…, and I will give you rest."

Almost before she got up from praying that prayer, she reached up and pulled one of those pearls from between His hands. Before the day was out, she had pulled out more and was worrying about them all over again. She said, "Immediately, I went back before the Lord and had to ask for forgiveness for not trusting Him to handle the problems I had just given Him. So, I gave them back to Him, placing those pearls back into His capable hands, again and again, because I thought God needed me to fix things He did not!

I am still learning to trust Him with the most secret troubles in my walk with the Lord. He can handle them if I do not take them back, and I trust Him to do so." She talked about growing in the Lord, maturing in Christ, and trusting Him to control each problem she gave Him.

She was an incredibly wise lady. Sadly, she was killed by a drunk driver only a couple of weeks after our conversation. She was killed by the very thing that she had fought so hard to overcome and did overcome! She was a great and mighty witness for our Lord.

When we give our troubles to God, we are to leave them there. But, so many times, I take them back from Him and again start trying to fix them by myself. Which is saying I don't trust God enough to leave them with him. I felt I must help God improve things. No, wrong, Gail! I know women are fixers, but sometimes it is just not our place.

In the book of Haggai, we are told of the fine houses the people had for themselves, and God's house lay in ruin. They were doing what they wanted to do instead of what God wanted. Haggai 1 tells us that God withheld His blessings upon the people because their hearts were not right with Him. He held back the dew, their crops did not produce, and He caused a drought upon the land.

I was doing what I wanted to do instead of what my Lord wanted. I tried to fix my marriage; I did not want to give what control I thought I had over to God. If I left, his drinking would worsen because he did not drink in front of me. With me there, it seemed to me as if he had stopped drinking. I thought he had stopped each time. But I'm afraid he only got worse as the years went on. When I would leave him, he would drink openly. I could not fix my marriage; Only God could.

We deceive ourselves when we say we are working for God when our heart is not right with Him. At first, Satan convinced me I was right. But God showed me that I was not listening to the Holy Spirit; I was not following God's will for my life. When this happened, I became responsible to God for my actions. It was easy to see my husband's faults and not even see my own. It is always easier to see someone else's fault than our own. I could no longer blame Satan for all my troubles. I had to put the blame where it belonged on my shoulders. I was the one who was living in sin.

Of course, what my husband was doing was wrong, but I could not answer for someone else. He alone had to answer for himself, as we all will. I could not fix him. Only God could. I am thankful God forgives and loves us, not based on what we do or do not do. He truly loves us. He forgives when we ask. I love that song; Jesus Loves Me

God wants us to be obedient to him, not a little of His will and a little of ours. Being committed to Him takes faith. I did not have enough faith in God to manage my problems. The Bible says, "Now faith is the substance of things hoped for, and the evidence of things not seen." (Hebrews 11:1). One example of faith is when we sit down in a chair. We have every confidence in that chair not to let us hit the floor. This is what I call blind faith—the kind we need to have in God.

We all struggle with trusting God to manage every situation that comes into our lives. Even the apostles ask the Lord to increase their faith. In Luke

17:5, the apostles, the men who walked with the Lord, needed more faith, and I know I sure do. There was an old song that said, 'Lord, keep me in your will so that I won't get in your way' this was indeed me. I was in God's way.

Satan wants to destroy any happiness we might have. I Peter 5:8 tells us he is roaming this earth seeking whom he may devour. There is no room for peace and happiness with stress and turmoil. When our minds are so focused on our troubles, we cannot have time to do God's will. Hebrews 11:6 God tells us that without faith, it is impossible to please Him. He also tells us to have faith in God in Mark 11:22. There is no better one to trust except the one who created us.

CHAPTER

Satan's Ways

*T*here are many ways in which Satan deceives us. First, Satan tries to keep a child of God from seeking God's will. He does not want us to recognize that God is the answer to the problem. Of course, as children of God, we know that. But we are still living in this sinful body. Sometimes we can get caught up in the circumstances without thinking we can leave God out of the equation. This can cause us to worry and stress because we don't know how to fix the problem. We begin to think about what it will take to correct what is happening so things can return to normal. This kind of stress can even keep us from sleeping at night.

We are not spending those sleepless nights saying, "Tonight, I think I will be disobedience to God." I think Satan keeps us in the dark about our disobedience. Satan is very deceitful! We may be unable to sleep because of some problems that we have not given to God. We may still be trying to manage them on our own. We cannot correct it until we recognize we sin against God by not letting Him have control. Satan does not want us to see what the solution is.

To step back and ask God to step into our lives takes faith. This can only strengthen our walk with Him. I am still striving for the day when I can give a problem to God, leave it there, and watch God at work. But as I walk with Him, this does get easier. As I walk with God and learn more about how to trust Him, my life is more manageable, and that sweet peace is in my life so much more often.

Our faith is tested when it is matters of the heart, like a loved one gone astray.

Satan also uses unforgiveness to keep distance between God and us. We all have had to deal with this at times in our lives. To be unforgiving is a sin. God said, in Matthew 6:14, "For if ye forgive men their trespasses, your heavenly Father will also forgive you." God said, "… pray for them that despitefully use you, and persecute you;" (Matthew 5:44). When

God says to do something, and we don't, it is a sin. He asks us to do some hard things, "...but with God, all things are possible." (Matthew 19:26)

Someone once said, "I have tried to forgive him, but you don't know how deeply he has hurt me. Just about the time I think I have forgiven him, here he comes, and he does something even meaner. It seems it never stops!" She was truly hurt very badly, and it wasn't just once. Only God could manage this kind of hurt. Please look to God and let him take your pain away; only He can.

People can be very mean with their words and how they treat others. Satan uses the pain caused by others to further his cause. He keeps reminding us of what they said about us and how they treated us. Satan needs to keep this pain alive. Because the longer we allow him to keep bringing this up in our minds, the longer we stay in sin by not forgiving. If we can't get over the hurt, we can't forgive.

One way to know if we have truly forgiven someone is to pray for them. I know this to be true. You cannot sincerely ask God to bless someone with His richest of blessings if you are still angry at them.

After being hurt so deeply, we don't want to see the one who hurt us prosper. That's human nature or the sinful nature we were born in. I thought for a long time that if you forgave someone, the wrong they had done to you would be as if they had done nothing wrong. This is not true.

When we forgive, we obey God's command. But God is still on the throne, and sin does not go unpunished. Whether it is your sin or mine, we all pay for our sins. "My son, despise not the chastening of the Lord; neither be weary of His correction: For whom the Lord loveth he correcteth; even as a father the son in whom he delighteth." (Proverbs 3:11–12)

It was explained to me this way. If a man murders another man and he goes to his family and tells them how sorry he was, and they forgive him, would there be no charges? Yes, there would be charges because there are laws of the land. He broke one of the laws by killing this man, and he must pay the price for it. So, he will be punished by spending time in jail or even being put to death.

God also has laws, commandments, or rules to live by. The one that did the offending which caused the hurt will not escape God's judgment. We must forgive as God said, or we will sin, and then we will have to answer for that! Only God has the authority to decide the punishment.

Satan also wants us to believe that it's ok for a man to marry a man and a woman to marry a woman. Everyone does that these days. I heard it said that God would not have made them that way and then want to destroy them as He did in Sodom. This is one of the worse deceptions of Satan today. In the book of Genesis, God made two sexes, male and female, and told them to populate the earth. God did not create a third sex for them to choose which one they want to be by having an operation. If so, that would make God a liar. God created all humanity, male and female, as told in Genesis 1:27 and Genesis 5:2. If a person chooses to become something else, they are sinning against God. To go against God is a dangerous thing.

A man and a man or a woman and a woman cannot make a baby. It takes one of each. In Genesis 19, God rained fire and sulfur from heaven on the cities named Sodom and Gomorrah because of this sin and because both cities were deep into different sins. Satan is exceptionally good at his job of deceiving us. We do not have to stay in our sin. Whatever kind of sin it is. God made way for us to rise above it.

We need forgiveness from God. His love for us is unconditional. We cannot be good enough to earn His favor. "As it is written, There is none righteous, no, not one." (Romans 3:10) But we can come before Him and ask for forgiveness, and that is all He asks of us, and our fellowship is restored.

To stay out of the sin we were in, we ask Him to give us strength and guide us in the way we should go. Once we get right with God again, Satan is trying to pull us back into our old ways. Always be on guard of him because I Peter 5:8 tells us he is like a roaring lion seeking whom he may devour. If we are not on guard and seeking the Lord daily, we can be pulled back into the same thing we just came out of.

I heard a story about a young woman living with a man who is the father of her sisters' children. Her sister said, "She felt very betrayed and could not believe this was real." Her sister responded, "I'm sure it is morally wrong, but I love him, and you can't help whom you love. But I hope someday we can all be friends again." Her sister, through streaming tears, said, "It's just so hard to explain all this to our twelve-year-old son." I do not think either woman was ever married to this man.

Satan can and does destroy so many lives daily. We are not to live together without marriage. We cannot go against God's laws and expect Him to bless us or help us when things go wrong. There are always consequences to sin. Asking for His forgiveness is the only way to restore that sweet fellowship.

CHAPTER

Standing on
The Promises

*G*od has made us so many promises that not even one event in this life can happen to us that God has not already made a way to escape. God will guide us on how to manage any problem or sin. But we must want help from Him and not our way. I have tried to solve my troubles on my own but not once has that worked out for me. His love for us is unconditional. All we must do is ask. He wants what is best for us. "The thief cometh not, but for to steal, and to kill, and to destroy: I am come that they might have life, and that they might have it more abundantly." (John 10:10). This means God has only good things in store for His children.

But when we step out of God's will for our life, we block the blessings He has for us, which is precisely what Satan wants us to do. Once we are saved, Satan cannot touch our souls, but he can influence our lives by pulling our thoughts away from God. He has ways of deceiving us. By tricking us into thinking, we can manage things on our own. Not one of us gets up in the morning and thinks that today, I will do things on my own and not ask God for help no matter what happens. Satan is much more subtle than that. When troubles come, things can begin to happen amazingly fast. This can create confusion for us all. Our instinct when we see something wrong is to try and help. Especially if the one hurting or about to get hurt is someone we love.

Unless we are close to God, He is not our first thought. Usually, our first thought is, what can I do? How can I fix this? This thinking, although human, can open the door for Satan to move into our lives. That is all he needs, an open door! When we can stay close to God and have faith, our first thought is, Dear God, if you can use me in this situation, please show me how to help. At that point, we know that God is in charge and is working all things for our good and His glory, as it says in Romans 8:28.

Faith is the hardest to have when it is tested. But it is also the most comforting during times of stress.

We may not always understand God's ways, but we walk by faith, not by what we see happening. "For we walk by faith, not by sight." (2 Corinthians 5:7). As we said, one thing Satan does not want a child of God to learn is how to live by faith. Because when we do, he cannot create havoc in our lives anymore. He cannot destroy our marriage or families when walking close to our heavenly Father. Things may not turn out the way we want. But they will be the way God wants, and therein lies our peace. People say we cannot live this way every day. Life is just too stressful and too fast-paced.

But God's peace and being close to Him is not something we put on only when needed, like a coat in the winter. It is, instead, a way of living. But it is the only way to live, and undoubtedly worth it. We never stop learning.

We are learning about God's ways and how He has told us to manage any situation that can come up. When we walk by faith, our hearts have a calm assurance. Because we know that whatever the outcome, it is in God's will, and his will is always best for us.

A man once told me that the Bible does not have an answer for everything. He said, "For example, if there is not enough money to go around and the rent is due. Then what? What happens when your boss always rides you, so you quit and can't find work anywhere? Does the Bible say to go to the hardware store and apply for a job? No, it doesn't," he said.

Sadly, I'm unsure if he ever took the time to learn how to stand on the promises before he died. I can tell you this; he was not a happy person. His life was spent complaining about the neighbors, the children, the cost of gasoline, and anything and everything. He assured me that he was saved and had a home in heaven. Salvation does not make our life all roses and sunshine. Salvation secures our home in heaven after death.

But following God after salvation makes life peaceful and fulfilling. We are responsible for learning to follow Him; when we don't, that is a sin. But Jesus said, "Trust in the Lord with all thine heart; and lean not to thine own understanding." (Proverbs 3:5)

To know how the bible answers each problem we face, we must study His Word and learn more about what He has for us. This is how we come to know and understand the peace of God. It takes time after salvation to learn more about God and who we are. It also takes studying God's word. It takes a lifetime. As we learn and grow, we become more like Him. "Study to show thyself approved…" (2 Timothy 2:15).

We all have things that we would rather not deal with. This is precisely what Satan wants, to keep us in the dark. Remember, when he spoke to Eve in the Garden of Eden, he even used God's words to tell her that if she ate the forbidden fruit, she would not surely die, as God had said in (Genesis 3:4). Eve did not know that it was Satan. But Eve was told what to do and what not to do. She knew right from wrong. Satan does not want us to know he is mixing in our lives, for if we knew it was Satan, we would not listen to him. When the Lord asked her what she had done, she said, "That the serpent had tricked her." That was no excuse; Eve knew right from wrong.

One thing is for sure; Satan has not changed. He still does not want us to know that he is anywhere around. Satan does not want us to see the truth because he is about destroying, and God is about restoring. But how to know that it is God speaking and not Satan? After all, Satan pretends to be Christ to get us to follow him. His name is Anti-Christ.

We must ask ourselves, is this what God would approve of? Try the spirits. "Beloved, believe not every spirit, but try the spirits whether they are of God: because many false prophets are gone out into the world." (I John 4:1). God warns us that things in this world can and do pull us away from Him.

Have you ever been to a casino or seen one on television? The colors, the bright lights, the music, the food, and the noise are all very inviting. Everyone seems to be having such a fun time. The things I have named are not bad, the lights, the music. But adding gambling and drinking in with this combination becomes a sin. This is no place for Jesus or a child of God. Because when we are saved and a child of the King, Jesus lives in our hearts. So, wherever we go, we take Jesus with us.

When we find ourselves in situations like this, we do not have to become part of it. Sin is attractive and inviting, whatever form it is in. I John 4:4 says, "Ye are of God, little children, and have overcome them: because greater is he that is in you than he that is in the world."

Scripture says for us to "… seek ye first, the kingdom of God…." (Matthew 6:33). So, we ask God to show us His way of managing whatever we face. We must put ourselves aside and accept whatever God's answer is. This is what is known as dying unto ourselves. Letting go of the way we want things to work out and yielding to God's way. Just because we ask God to show us the path does not mean we will follow it. This takes faith, "So, then faith cometh by hearing, and hearing by the word of God." (Romans 10:17)

Read God's word and listen to the preaching of His word. God has called men to preach His Word, so we are to listen. However, we need to be careful about whom we listen to. Matthew 7:15 says, "Beware of false prophets, which come to you in sheep's clothing, but inwardly they are ravening wolves." Not all men that preach are really of God. One way to know is by listening and seeing if what they say is in line with the word of God. If it is not, then run away and find one who is. Because if we stay in something that we know is not of God, then this is willful sin. One we will answer for.

Sadly, some places are called churches, and God's word is not being taught inside. Satan goes to church, too, you know. Have you ever sat in church thinking angry thoughts about someone you can't forgive? What will we have for lunch, or where will we go after church? Being distracted is one of Satan's tools.

If our hearts are not set for worship before we get to church, we may just be bringing Satan with us to the very house of God. We must not only get our bodies dressed for church but our hearts as well. I'm sure you have been to church and gotten home and thought, I have done my duty for God this week, and then there are times when we leave the church and can hardly wait to return. It was so good. We cannot stop talking about how excellent the service was and what a great message he preached.

The preacher cannot prepare our hearts for worship. Only we can. One of the best ways is to pray for the preacher as he prepares for the next service. Preachers have a formidable responsibility to tell us what God has laid on his heart for us to hear. They need our prayers daily. To get our hearts ready, we must look for God's will for our lives through prayer and study, and by the time we get to church on Sunday, we are prepared to worship our creator.

When we genuinely search for God's will, the Holy Spirit will lead us in the ways we should go.

When I was searching for a church home, I visited different churches. I knew I was in a scriptural church, but in my heart, I knew this was not where God wanted me to be. Then one Sunday, I was visiting this church, and in my heart, I knew this was where God wanted me. I had peace in my heart.

After asking God for guidance for a church home or help with any problem, we must do our part by continuing to seek His will for our lives. Read His Word daily and pray that the answer will come in His time. His time is not our time.

If you are like me, you want an answer right now, please. But our God doesn't always work like that. He has other factors going on that we don't even know about, and when He has everything in place just like He wants, our answer will come. Sometimes, we can ask for something, and the answer comes at once. We are to have faith in Him and stand on those 32,000 promises that God has made us. Only God.

CHAPTER

One Foot in Front of The Other

*M*y husband had a massive heart attack ten years before he passed away. He would never work again; it had left him disabled. Now we had to adjust to our new way of living with him being home all the time, and I had to get a second job. My Mom, whom I dearly loved, had broken her hip and now was close by at a rehab center so I could see her daily.

One day I took off work to take my husband back to see the doctor. As the doctor examined him, I found a chair in the corner of the room. About halfway through her examination, the doctor said, "Sir, I will be back with you in just a minute." I looked up, and she was walking towards me. She continued, "I would not be much of a doctor if I didn't at least address your wife. You see, Sir, your wife is an extremely sick lady." She reached down, moved my bangs to one side, and said, "See, just look in her eyes." I sat there in complete shock! I knew I was tired, but I worked two jobs, caring for a sick husband and my mother. I thought I had a right to be this tired.

"Please, do not leave my office without at least letting me examine you and draw blood," she said. I looked across the room at my husband as if to say what I should do. He just shrugged his shoulders. Again, the doctor looked at me and said, "Please, allow me to put you in another exam room, and when I finish with him, I will be right in." As shocked as I was, I agreed. A nurse came in and took me to another room. How often does this happen? Only God!

When the doctor came in, I asked about my husband, and she assured me he would be fine. He just needed antibiotics. Then I asked what she thought was wrong with me. As doctors do, she said, "We will know more in a day or two when these results come in. I think you may have internal problems."

Two days later, the doctor called; she thought something was wrong with my liver. I was to contact my doctor and go from there.

I did, and after my doctor went over all this information and tests of her own, she told me I would have to see a specialist, and we had two options in two different towns. The doctor recommended one, and I wanted to go to the other one. The one I wanted would be closer to us. But we agreed that whomever they could get an appointment with first would be where I would go.

She said I needed to be seen right away. When she first told me what was wrong with me, I just sat silently, trying to understand her words. I'm not sure how long that was, but when I came back to myself, I realized that this very busy doctor had sat silently with me. I looked at her and could see her compassion for me. We discussed how God was in charge. However, this turned out. She is one great doctor.

I went home waiting to hear. One day the phone rang, and the specialists called from out of state. These people were not even one of the two my doctor and I had discussed. Only God could send me to the right set of doctors; He had a plan. He was sending me to the place where He wanted me to go. Appointments were made, and tests were scheduled. The weeks that followed were exhausting. The hospital where all this was being done was about a two-hour drive. I worked as much as I could as finances were getting a little tight. It was amazing. There was always enough. Only God could provide in this way. With all the testing and my being away from home so often, my husband started drinking again.

I found it harder and harder to put one foot in front of the other. Now he was complaining all the time. It seemed all we did was argue about everything! As the days went by, I was getting weaker and did not have the strength for all this fussing.

One thing led to another, and I had to leave. I had to find a quiet place. By this time in our life, our children were out of the house, making their own families. It had been a long journey. I took an apartment in town. I kept praying he would change, especially now.

One afternoon I went to see my mother. Mom said, "When will you tell me what is wrong? I know you are sick." Moms can look at their children and know. I always tried to avoid that conversation with her. She had enough to worry about.

Not long after that, mom fell, broke the other hip, and was taken to the hospital. So, I packed a bag and stayed the night in the hospital with her. Surgery was to be the next morning. They came early the next day and took her away. The surgery went well, and everything was fine. She would be going back to rehab in a day or two. My sisters were there, so I went home and rested for a while. It wasn't long before I got a call to get back over there. Something was wrong.

After I arrived, it was only a couple of hours later that my precious Mother went to be with our Lord. This couldn't be true, but it was! Not my mom! Only God could get me through this, and He did. I was so blessed to have had a genuinely Godly woman as a mother. She taught me so much about our Creator.

I could not believe she was gone. But later, I was thankful my mom did not have to witness what I was about to go through. That was a blessing.

I could not imagine how happy my mom was now. I will always miss her while I am left on this earth. But someday soon, I will join her. She was the greatest!

CHAPTER

Two Weeks Left to Live

*F*inally, all those test results were in. Even though I never drank alcohol, I had cirrhosis of the liver. They called it Primary Biliary Non-Acholic Cirrhosis of the liver. I had end-stage liver disease! What? How could this be?

They told me you are malnourished and not strong enough to be placed on the transplant list. At this point, I thought, transplant list? Am I that bad off? I thought they would give me some new medicine and go home.

I was sent home to eat lots of eggs for protein and get my strength built up, or I would die. When and if I got stronger, then we would see.

Well, here I was. I was living apart from my husband for forty-plus years. He was sick and needed me, or so I thought. My sweet Mom has just gone home to heaven, and now I have a deadly disease I cannot even spell!

I worked as much as possible; by this time, I had lost over fifty pounds. It was tough to eat anything. A sweet friend showed me how to make protein-enriched smoothies, which helped build me back up.

They had told me at the hospital that I would have to fill out a Medical Power of Attorney because I would be placed on a ventilator after surgery. Then they asked if I was married. Yes, I was, but we are not together, I told them. That did not matter. We were still married. If you are married, the spouse has authority over you in situations like this. He had the right to say what would happen to me. I had been gone over a year now, and he had only gotten worse with the drinking instead of better.

I had prayed about what to do about that medical power, and now my answer was clear I could not allow him that kind of authority over me. He was in no shape to decide this. His thinking just wasn't correct and getting worse. I had no choice but to take this power away from him.

The only way to do that was to divorce him! I could not believe this, not now!

I knew in my heart I would never return if I were ever strong enough to divorce him. So now God gave me no choice. God will allow us to stay in sin if we want, but there is a payday; this was mine.

I wish I had listened to those gentle nudges from the Holy Spirit much earlier. Because now it would be just God and him.

I had put what I wanted first. I wanted a good marriage. I did not desire a bad thing; every woman wants a good marriage. But I did not have my priorities straight; it is God first, then everything else will fall into place. "But seek ye first the kingdom of God, and His righteousness; and all these things shall be added unto you." (Matthew 6:33). I knew this, but my stubbornness was hard to let go of. God wants to be first in our lives, only God.

Even though God had to punish or discipline me for not trusting Him to control my marriage, God is sovereign. He is always right and always fair. He never once left me through any of this.

When we had to punish our children for something they had done wrong, we did not turn our back on them because they disobeyed! If they were grounded for a week during that week, we still fed and loved them just the same. But there had to be a payday for their disobedience—the same with God. God had to discipline me because of His great love for me, as in (Proverbs 3:11–12).

God was not judging, nor was he placing judgment on me. He was correcting me as we do our children.

Numbers 12:1–12 tell us when Miriam spoke against Moses. God used a skin affliction called leprosy to correct her. God does whatever He knows is necessary to restore His children and bring them back to where we need to be.

As it says in Romans 8:28, "...All things work together for good...." God had dealt with me earlier to let him have complete control, but I did not have enough faith. So, when my correction came, I knew why. Not every time a person gets sick is that punishment or correction from God. No one has the right to say you have this awful disease or cancer, and now you are paying for your sins. That would be judging. Only God is the judge. His word says, "Judge not, that ye be not judged." (Matthew 7:1). However, I knew why this was happening to me. I have been told that if one receives correction from God, only that individual knows for sure. I have also heard that if you have never felt the chastening hand of the Lord, you must examine your life. As it says in Proverbs 3:12. God chastens those He loves.

In John 9:2–3, there was a man born blind, and the disciples thought either that he or someone in his family must have sinned. God told them no; I have another reason for his blindness from birth. God is sovereign.

For correction, God may use sickness, financial worries, or any number of things. Only God knows how to correct His children. We are all different, and I am sure it would take many different types of correction. Only God has the right to decide this.

A woman once told me she had cancer. She said it was the best thing that ever happened to her.

Because it brought her closer to God, where she found peace and contentment. I now know what she meant. I am thankful He loved me enough to get me back into the center of His will for my life. He never gave up on me.

If we are a child of God and do not obey what God has told us to do, He will put us back on the right path. It may take a while, or His discipline may come quickly. Rest assured, it will come. He loves us, and He wants what is best for us.

Once I held a job that was working with minor children from broken homes. Some were in foster care. During the day, we had to correct the children. I remember how they would hug my neck before going home. Even though hours earlier, I had to put them in the corner for something they had done. Those children knew they were loved. Discipline means love. They did not like the punishment, but they knew we cared.

I did not like my punishment. But I knew it was for my good and that I was loved. God was leading me to the dawn of a new day.

Truthfully, I was finally right with God. All the way, my will was broken and gone. That is a great feeling. Nothing between my soul and my Savior, as the old song says. I finally surrendered my will to His; the blessings have been untold for me since then. We will always have trials to go through on this earth. But with God on our side, each one is easier to face.

I never stopped caring and praying for my husband. I felt a great responsibility was lifted from my shoulders, but it was one I had placed there. It was not mine to carry. I wanted my husband to find what I had seen in God, complete peace. But this time, I was allowing God to take the lead.

One day as I was getting dressed for Church, I noticed my skin seemed to have a nice tan color. I wondered about it, I sure hadn't been sunbathing, but it was time for Church. So, I ignored it.

A week later, my nice tan had turned yellow from head to toe. The whites of my eyes were even yellow. I was jaundiced! Before it was over, I became a bright yellow! People stared! I could feel myself growing weaker daily.

Betty and I have been best friends since Jr. High school. She is indeed a blessing from God. She has always been there for me. She loves God with all her heart, so when I asked for her advice, I knew she gave me Godly wisdom. One afternoon we were out shopping. I wanted to talk with Betty about this business of a transplant. I had wrestled with this whether to have it done or not. Someone else's organ in my body? Besides, that would mean someone would have to die for me to live.

I told Betty, "You know I'm dying?" Betty said, "Yes, I know." I said, "I have decided to have the surgery, but chances of that happening are exceedingly rare. But if it is God's will for my life, then it will happen. I am not struggling with the decision anymore. I have given it all to God." She was glad I was finally at peace about it. We finished our visit, and each went back home. We lived in different towns.

It was not 15 minutes after I started home that my phone rang, and it was the Transplant Team!

I answered the phone, and the lady said, "We have a match for you. How fast can you get here?"

My reply, with tears streaming, "I know you do."
Only God.

The tears that ran down my face were not because I had a chance to keep living. But I knew that whatever happened, God was with me. I was not afraid.

After the surgery, the doctors told me it was worse than they thought. I had only two weeks left to live. That was almost five years ago. Only God.

CHAPTER

Forgetting The Past

I am sure you have read about Saul and how he persecuted the Christians. He had people put to death. But it is believed that Saul himself did not kill anyone. He approved when Stephen was stoned to death according to Acts 7:58–8:1. Then, in Acts 9:2, Saul was going to Damascus and asked if he could have letters giving him the right to arrest any Christian he saw on his way. Saul was a very well-educated man, but he made havoc on the church. He would also go into people's homes, taking men, women, or children and having them thrown into prison, as it says in Acts 8:3.

He despised the disciples. As Saul went down the road, a light shone from heaven. Saul fell to the ground and heard a voice from heaven say, "…Saul,

Saul, why persecutes thou me?" (Acts 9:4). Jesus did not need to ask Saul this question. He knew the answer. But through their conversation, Saul found Jesus as his Savior that day! He was blinded that day but was obedient to the Lord, and his sight was returned in three days.

I cannot imagine the obstacles that he faced as he went about preaching about our Lord. The Jews now wanted him dead because he was no longer against the Christians. The disciples feared him because of what he had done to them and their families, as told in Acts 9:26.

But Saul had found Jesus and now knew what to do. God used this man in mighty ways to bring His message to the world we live in today. Satan had blinded his eyes, but Saul saw the truth for the first time when God blinded them.

Out of the twenty-seven books of the New Testament, God inspired Paul (God later changed Saul's name to Paul) to write fourteen of them. If we surrender ourselves to Him, what could we do for God? I have known Godly men and women, and I love being around them.

We are not perfect yet, not until we get to Heaven. We all have things in our past that we feel are best forgotten. As hard as it was, I have told you of <u>one</u>, of my disobedience to our Lord.

Our sins must be faced, not overlooked, because trust me when I tell you that you cannot forget, without first asking Him for forgiveness, then you can. God is our creator. He knows all about our weaknesses, flaws, secrets, and thoughts.

He says, "Come unto me all ye that labor and are heavy laden, and I will give you rest." (Matthew 11:28). "If we confess our sins, he is faithful and just to forgive us our sins, and to cleanse us from all unrighteousness." (I John 1:9)

Not only does He forgive us, but He also cleanses us, and our fellowship with Him is restored. Peace again! Do not allow Satan another day, hour, minute, or second to steal what is left of your precious time listening to his lies by telling us to forget about the past. It is over. It is not over until we have asked for forgiveness and are right with God again.

We know our sins must be dealt with. Remember, Satan wants to keep us in the dark, but God wants us to live in the light.

Paul said in Philippians 3:13, "...but this one thing I do, forgetting those things which are behind, and reaching forth unto those things which are before,"

Even Jesus said, "As far as the east is from the west, so far hath He removed our transgressions from us." (Psalm 103:12)

I do not know how far it is from the east to the west. But I know that if Jesus removes my sins that far away from me and God has forgiven me, who am I not to forgive myself? Redemption!

Our past mistakes can no longer keep us in bondage. There is freedom in forgiveness. That forgiveness can come from only God!

CHAPTER

Undeserved Blessings

*O*ne of the first blessings that come to mind is that Jesus saved my soul when I was eleven. He has never left me since. Always with me. When my dear Mom passed away from this life and entered heaven, He allowed me to be by her bedside. He also allowed me to be with the love of my life when he drew his last breath; I was holding his hand. I know he is at peace with our Lord today, with no more struggles.

God has given me two beautiful daughters, two remarkable sons-in-law, two precious grandchildren, and five sweetest great-grandchildren. If I lived another hundred years, I could never name all the blessings God has given me. His love for sinners like me is fantastic. His forgiveness is incredible. His faithfulness is steadfast.

The following are things we all face and where to find the help we need.

Worrying? Worry is to give way to anxiety to allow one's mind to dwell on difficulty or troubles.

With today's fast-paced life, I am afraid worry has become all too much a part of our lives. It can rob us of a good night's sleep and create incredibly stressful days. But it does not have to be this way. Philippians 4:6 says "Be careful for nothing…" and Psalm 37:7 says "…fret not thyself…" My Mom would say that when we are worrying, we are not trusting God. I knew when she said it that she was right. But I was still worried. Because truthfully, I was not trusting God.

Peaceful? Free from disturbance: tranquil.

I know that at times in our lives, we have had that beautiful, peaceful moment. But this kind of peace is one we can have daily. There are at least four hundred-twenty verses in the Bible that refer to peace. One of my favorites is John 14:27, "Peace I leave with you, my peace I give unto you: not as the world giveth, give I unto you. Let not your heart be troubled, neither let it be afraid."

Loving? Agape love is the love of humanity.

We know what it is to be in love with another or to love your children. But this kind of love can only come from God through us to others. We are to be more like Him. "He that loveth not, knoweth not God; for God is love." (I John 4:8). He wants us first to love Him and then love our neighbor just like we love ourselves. No commandment greater than these, says Mark 12:30–31. Have you ever loved your neighbor as yourself? Of course, we have loved our family this way, but what about that neighbor? God said this is one of His greatest commandments. He also said, "If ye love me, keep my commandments." (John 14:15). How in the world could we possibly love that old guy next door that is always watching us or always wanting to know who came to visit us? We can't! But with Jesus, we can! "But Jesus beheld them, and said unto them, With men this is impossible, but with God all things are possible." (Matthew 19:26)

Careful of our words.

"Keep thy tongue from evil, and thy lips from speaking guile." (Psalm 34:13). This is an area where we all can show improvement. Our words can lift someone out of depression and comfort during grief or sadness, or we can tear someone down. To hurt someone with our words is a horrible thing to do. It can happen so quickly unless we are on guard with our words. We do not know what another person is going through and sometimes how our words can affect them. "Let your speech be alway with grace, seasoned with salt, that ye may know how ye ought to answer every man." (Colossians 4:6)

Anger? A strong feeling of being upset or annoyed because of something wrong or bad: that feeling that makes someone want to hurt other people, to shout.

"Wherefore, my beloved brethren, let every man be swift to hear, slow to speak, slow to wrath:" (James 1:19). "Make no friendship with an angry man; and with a furious man thou shalt not go:" (Proverbs 22:24) "Be ye angry, and sin not: let not the sun go down upon your wrath:" (Ephesians 4:26)

We have all been angry. It is ok to be angry, but as it says, be angry and sin not. Do not let our anger guide us so much that we lose control and commit sin against God. Not one of us is above sin. We all sin daily. "If we say that we have no sin, we deceive ourselves, and the truth is not in us." (I John 1:8)

I know we all have that place where we like to go and think about things and talk with the Lord. Mine has always been the water. When things got too bad, I would go fishing or go to the lake for peace if possible. Being near the water always helps me to think more clearly.

Today because of God's grace, love, mercy, and forgiveness, not because of anything I have done. I can sit in my living room, look out the window and see the ducks swimming in the cove. I can walk across the road and go fishing or sit on the porch swing, see the fish jump, and listen to the wind in the trees. He showed me this wonderful rental house over a year ago.

My church is nearby; my neighbors are caring and loving. I could not ask for better landlords. I have peace. Only God.

I am still a sinner, saved by grace. But, as I travel the rest of my journey homeward, with our Lord's help, I am learning how to walk with God daily.

I can hardly wait to get to Heaven if life can be this good on earth. See you there.

May God bless you and your families on your journey homeward.

Printed in the United States
by Baker & Taylor Publisher Services